Da...   now

Dashing Through

The Story of the Jr. Iditarod

the Snow

Sherry Shahan

The Millbrook Press
Brookfield, Connecticut

An avalanche of appreciation to the Fielder family for sharing their magical winter wonderland: Linwood, Kathi, Christi, and especially Dalton. And gratitude to John King, dog handler extraordinaire.

Published by
The Millbrook Press, Inc.
2 Old New Milford Road
Brookfield, Connecticut 06804

Library of Congress Cataloging-in Publication Data
Shahan, Sherry.
Dashing through the snow: the story of the Jr. Iditarod /Sherry Shahan.
p. cm.
Includes index.
Summary: Presents the history and action of the Junior Iditarod, the annual dogsled race for young people in Alaska, discussing such related topics as dog care, equipment, and technique.
ISBN 0-7613-0208-5 (lib. bdg.)   0-7613-0143-7 (pbk)
1. Junior Iditarod Trail Sled Dog Race, Alaska—Juvenile literature. [1. Junior Iditarod Trail Sled Dog Race, Alaska. 2. Sled dog racing.] I. Title.
SF440.15.S53 1997
798'.8—dc20   96-27075   CIP   AC

Introduction

The year was 1925. It seemed as if the unrelenting snowstorm might blow the frozen Alaska territory into the Bering Sea. All trails were as deep and thick as a mug of miner's coffee and just as slow to go down.

Yet news traveled with lightning speed: Countless numbers of Eskimo children in Nome had been exposed to the highly infectious disease diphtheria, also known as "black death." The Alaska Railroad Hospital in Anchorage stocked the only serum in the territory. How could it be transported to icebound Nome, more than 1,000 miles (1,600 kilometers) away, in the shortest possible time?

In 1925 flying small airplanes was risky business. Could a bush plane operate at -40°F? No one knew. And if the plane didn't make it, neither would the life-saving serum.

An alternative plan was offered: The serum would travel by railroad to Nenana, then be transported to Nome by dog team in the ancient tradition

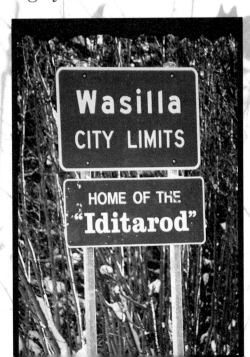

Wasilla, Alaska, is the starting point of the Jr. Iditarod Sled Dog Race.

5

of Native Alaskans who mastered the art of using dogs for winter transportation. In relay style, twenty fearless mushers and their teams of hard-driving huskies carried the serum 647 miles (1,178 kilometers) in 127 ½ hours, almost 5 ½ days.

Blizzard conditions sometimes pushed the windchill factor to -100°F (-73°C). The serum arrived frozen, but still usable.

During these years sled-dog teams were called on to transport mail, supplies, and people. Gold miners traveled to remote goldfields, and the precious ore was carted out by dogsled. Later, airplanes took over the mail routes, and the gold rush slowed down. Snow machines eventually sped onto the scene, pushing the tradition of dog sledding closer to extinction.

The 1,049-mile (1,688-kilometer) Iditarod Trail Sled Dog Race was organized in 1973 by mushing enthusiasts who were saddened by the declining use of dogsleds. Much more than a race, the event is a commemoration of the heroic 1925 "serum run" from Anchorage to Nome.

Today, dogsledding is a popular sport in cold climates around the world. It is just as popular in Alaska as football or baseball is in the lower 48 states, but the playing field is a million square miles (2.6 million square kilometers). Dog mushing now claims the title "Official State Sport" of Alaska.

In 1977 the Jr. Iditarod was started to enable mushers between the ages of fourteen and seventeen, male and female, to compete in a two-day version of "The Last Great Race on Earth." The junior route is shorter, approximately 150 miles (240 kilometers), but it demands just as much training and skill of mushers and dog teams. Rookies as well as veterans confront endless challenges as they mush into the untamed wilderness and down a trail laid with a rich historic past.

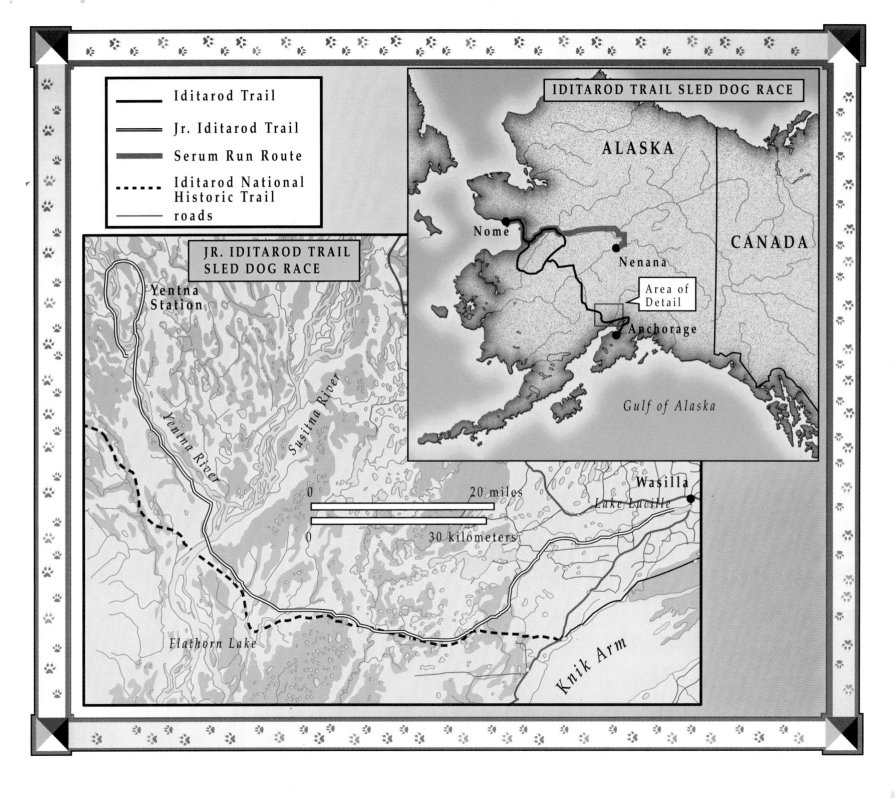

Iditarod Trail

Jr. Iditarod Trail

Serum Run Route

Iditarod National Historic Trail

roads

JR. IDITAROD TRAIL SLED DOG RACE

Yentna Station

Yentna River

Susitna River

Flathorn Lake

Knik Arm

Wasilla

Lake Lucille

0   20 miles

0   30 kilometers

IDITAROD TRAIL SLED DOG RACE

ALASKA

CANADA

Nome

Nenana

Area of Detail

Anchorage

Gulf of Alaska

Opposite: *After the team, a musher's sled is his or her most important piece of equipment.*

Below: *A sled dog waits in its compartment to be hitched to the rest of the team.*

A line of dog trucks with camperlike shells flash their bright taillights, carefully pulling onto the frozen lake. The unsettling sound of cracking ice sinks under the deafening barks, yips, and howls of more than a hundred huskies. After many months of training, the dogs are eager to hear the words, "Hike!" or "All right!"

It is 8:30 A.M., the last Saturday in February. The official start of the Jr. Iditarod Trail Sled Dog Race is one and a half hours away. A bundled crowd shivers in the icy subzero temperatures: Race officials, dog handlers, veterinarians, friends, and relatives are all here.

The mushers themselves are too busy to feel the cold. Each dog in their team is unloaded from its compartment in the dog box, which is custom-fit on the bed of a pickup truck. Gear is gathered up and packed in sled bags. Padded harnesses are slipped over the dogs' heads,

11

followed by, "How're you doing, fella?" Frozen fish is tossed on the ice as a prerace snack. With minutes ticking away, tuglines and necklines are snapped to the main line, called a gangline.

One at a time, mushers ease their teams into the starting chute under the fluttering Jr. Iditarod banner. Teams are announced over a public-address system and released at staggered, two minute intervals: " . . . two-time winner Tim Osmar from

Clam Gulch, Alaska . . . ." Well-wishers and clicking cameras follow racing bibs as the numbers disappear into the vast white wilderness.

All entrants in the Jr. Iditarod attended a special meeting the night before the race at Iditarod Headquarters in Wasilla, Alaska. During the meeting a flood of questions about the trail were asked and answered. Starting positions were drawn from a hat. Racing bibs and maps of the route were handed

out. Earlier in the day, all dogs were carefully examined by a veterinarian. Current immunization records were reviewed before the official health certificate was signed.

Just off his snow machine and still in grease-covered overalls, a trailbreaker described the wooden stakes that mark the route. Tagged with strips of bright plastic or reflecting tape, the stakes clearly mark the trail before and after every turn. These guides are especially important during wind-driven blizzards, when snow can erase any trace of the trail.

The teenage veterans and rookies alike squirmed in their chairs, knowing that the race takes place during the coldest season in the frozen north. "Don't like the weather?" a rookie says, "Wait five minutes."

This old-time saying characterizes the constantly changing, always unpredictable winter weather conditions in Alaska: blizzards can cut visibility to zero, gale-force winds slice through heavy parkas, and temperatures often drop to -30°F (-34°C) or below.

The meeting ended with "Good luck!" to all the mushers.

Mushers drive their teams toward the halfway point, Yentna Station Roadhouse, about 75 miles (120 kilometers) from the start. There's no such thing as a foolproof race plan. Every musher's strategy has to be as flexible as the constantly changing trail and weather conditions. In deep snow, teams "swim" down the trail in slow, clumsy movements. On a hard, well-packed trail a musher holds a team down to 10 to 12 miles (16 to 18 kilometers) per hour to keep them from running too fast. No matter what the trail conditions may be, pacing is everything.

An empty basket sled weighs between 30 and 40 pounds (13.5 and 18 kilograms). But a sled loaded down with gear and dog food is twice that heavy and can be more difficult to steer. Mushers constantly shift their body weight as their team maneuvers ditches, boulders, trees, and sled-busting twists and turns.

The stretch of the trail from Lake Lucille to Yentna Station Roadhouse is known as "Moose Alley." In years of very heavy snowfall, moose encounters present a serious threat. Rather than trudge through deep snow, the animals, which can weigh 1,000

pounds (450 kilograms) or more, travel the paths of least resistance: roads, railroad tracks, and sled dog trails. Horror stories of huskies being killed in moose attacks cause mushers to scan the terrain for any sign of the animals, preparing to drop the snow hook and stop the team. Moose are always given the right-of-way.

Mushers stand with legs wide apart, each boot balanced on a sled runner. The handlebar is gripped tightly in the face of wind-whipped snow and hairpin turns.

In extreme cold, heat packs are slipped inside gloves and boots. Some mushers sew special pockets in the top of their long underwear for the air-activated packs. Neck gaiters cover both nose and mouth. Warm breath forms condensation, and the gaiters freeze. But the boots are so heavily insulated that some mushers don't even wear socks unless it's -30°F (-34°C) or colder.

The voices of mushers calling dog names like "Atta Boy" and "Wolfie" echo on the trail, and dog ears prick at the

sound. Since sled dogs aren't reined like a team of horses, the musher's only control is through verbal commands. "Gee" and "haw" called out to the two dogs at the head of the team, known as lead dogs, translate into right- and left-turn commands. "All right!" and "Hike!" mean "Let's go!" "Mush!," though hardly ever used, comes from the French word *marchon,* which means "to walk."

Older dogs in the team teach the younger members trail etiquette. But sometimes

bad habits are also taught, such as chewing on booties and tangling lines. If one of the lead dogs starts to slow down, a new dog is shifted to a front spot in less than 60 seconds, including the unsnapping and resnapping of lines. With a new leader up front the team often picks up its pace.

After hours of mushing down the Iditarod National Historic Trail and over several frozen lakes, the Jr. Iditarod route swings wide across Flat Horn Lake. Every year at

20

Mandatory Gear List

The following items must be in a musher's possession at all times:

- Cold-weather sleeping bag
- Cold-weather clothes and boots
- Ax with a handle at least 22 inches (56 centimeters) long
- Pair of snowshoes with bindings
- Iditarod Trail Committee promotional material
- Headlamp and an additional battery-powered light
- Eight booties for each dog, either in use or in the sled
- Some type of restraint to hold a dog (or dogs) in the sled, if necessary
- Lighter or matches to start a fire
- Dog-food cooker

- Three stake-out cables or chains (minimum 6 inches [40 centimeters] long with snaps at each end) to be used for staking a dropped dog

Rules require mandatory dog food to be in the sled at each checkpoint.

Optional items carried in the sled:

- Tent
- Camp stove
- Feed pans for dogs
- Cooking pans for musher
- Fuel for stove
- Waterproof ground cloth

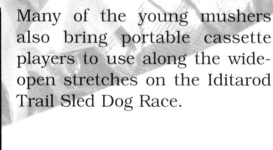

Many of the young mushers also bring portable cassette players to use along the wide-open stretches on the Iditarod Trail Sled Dog Race.

least one of the young dog drivers loses sight of the trail markers here. Time lost while a musher zigzags over the ice searching for the race route is gone forever. Sometimes hours pass before a stake is spotted and the team is back on track.

Beyond Flat Horn Lake mushers shout "Whoa!" and tromp on the drag brake, a flat metal contraption with claws. The sharp claws dig into snow and ice, reinforcing the verbal command to stop. The team and driver rest briefly at a "pass through" checkpoint, untangling lines and replacing booties while an official checks off mandatory gear.

The dogs bark loudly and jump straight up in their harnesses, eager to get going again. Mushers sign in and out at this checkpoint, which is the only official stop between Wasilla and Yentna Station. Snow flies off paws, and tails curl over backs, as each team takes off.

Now the late afternoon sun falls behind a mountain range, and temperatures dip even lower. Farther down the trail it's time for a snack. Most mushers "snack" their

23

teams every two hours during the race. The first snack might be hearty chunks of raw lamb, beaver, or "ends and pieces" of human-grade bacon.

The next one might be a "wet" snack, a soupy mixture of water and crumbled commercial dog food. This wet feed is a tasty, watery mixture that baits dogs to drink. Keeping a dog team hydrated, or watered, is as important as fueling it with solid food.

Temperatures determine the type of food snacked. If it is "hot" outside (10 to 20°F, or -12 to -7°C), a musher tosses

out frozen chunks of fish, maybe salmon or herring. Since fish is mostly water, it helps with hydration. If it's cold—for example, -20°F (-29°C) or below, a thawed chunk of meat is offered.

Some mushers concoct high-energy dog snacks called "honeyballs." About the size of a chicken egg, a honeyball is a mixture of fatty meat, powdered eggs, honey, oil, and vitamins. Some add bonemeal, brewer's yeast, and commercial dog food. Since the ingredients are all mixed up, honeyballs are easy to digest.

Booties

"All bootied up and ready to go!"

A dog bootie is a snug-fitting sock designed to protect paws and toe pads from rough trails. Each musher has a favorite material for the homemade booties. Although most use a soft fabric such as polar fleece, trigger cloth, or denim, others have turned to sturdier nylon. Unlike fleece, nylon sheds snow and water. Nylon is also slicker so snow doesn't ball up as easily. A Velcro strap helps keep booties in place. Still, dozens of the colorful socks litter the trail.

If the trail is rough with ice and temperatures are subzero, booties can wear out in less than 10 miles (16 kilometers). A musher can spend up to two hours a day on bootie care alone. Rules require mushers to carry "eight booties for each dog, either in the sled or in use and in the sled."

Mushers are always watching the dozens of feet trotting in front of the sled. Even a subtle change in a dog's gait can signal bootie problems. Booties starting to slip, or booties with holes, are quickly adjusted or changed—snow can work its way through the smallest opening and form irritating ice balls.

Every musher knows that the old saying is true: "A dog team is only as good as its feet."

Opposite: *Mushing is hard work.*
After snacking, both musher and
team take a quick nap.

Below: *It can get lonely on the trail,*
but mushers have much to think
about and much to be aware of.

A working sled dog can burn up to 10,000 calories a day. Much of the talk on the trail centers around dog food. "It's too hot and the liver is starting to thaw." Or, "I hope the turkey skins are still solid."

Hours peel away as snow begins to fall. Long straightaways of the frozen river seem to go on forever. Sometimes the only sound is the faint *whoosh* of sled runners on ice.

To ease their boredom, mushers often carry portable cassette players with headphones. The music is intended to keep them alert, but at

least one musher usually falls asleep standing on the runners. Tumbling off a sled is an instant wake-up call—so is scrambling after a team in heavy snow.

Constantly watching the team for signs of fatigue, the drivers race across a wide section of tree-lined Susitna River. The route follows the Yentna River to the halfway point of the race, Yentna Station Roadhouse.

A heavy snowfall sets a wintry scene for this rustic way station on the banks of Yentna River in the Susitna Valley, population 8.

Since the only roads to Yentna Station are frozen rivers, this out-of-the-way checkpoint usually limits visitors to race officials, the race veterinarian and doctor, one ham radio operator, and sometimes a few photographers. The radio operator keeps track of teams on the trail, providing race updates and relaying messages.

Non-mushers arrive at Yentna in small bush planes flown by volunteer pilots, called the "Jr. Iditarod Air Force." A line of twigs hammered into ice marks a makeshift runway where the planes land.

Many teams mush into Yentna Station Roadhouse after dark with only the narrow beams of their headlamps lighting the way. They arrive at different times, some of the teams separated by more than two hours. The front-runners and tail-enders might be as much as five hours apart.

The race marshal leads each team to its own parking spot in the trees. More than one dog arrives inside a sled, its head poking out of the sled bag. These "dropped" dogs leave the race for different reasons, usually minor injuries, illness, or fatigue.

The decision to drop a dog is an act of caring and kindness. It's also a sacrifice since a dog carried inside the sled adds extra weight and slows down the team—often negatively affecting the team's position in the race. Once a dog is dropped, it is permanently withdrawn from the race, and another dog can't be substituted in its place.

A veterinarian examines all the dogs under a generator-powered light in the front yard of the roadhouse. Dropped dogs receive medical treatment in a special area and are tethered to trees until the return flight home.

Mushers "park" their team, then step stiffly off sled runners and wrap the snub line around a tree. Inside the lodge, wet outer clothes hang around the wood-burning stove. Frozen sweat is shaken from boot-liners. Dry gloves replace wet ones. The mushers themselves don't have time to enjoy the fire. Back outside, hours of hard work lie ahead.

A bale of straw is broken into flakes and spread on the ground, providing each dog with its own thick bed. Mushers check their dogs' feet for swelling or small splits in the webs of their

31

paws, and ointment is dabbed on as needed. Shoulders and hips are massaged. Ankle wraps keep dog muscles warm.

Time is spent with each member of the team to discuss the day's ups and downs. The dogs have their own personalities: Some thump their tails, others roll on their backs. Tails wag and mushers' cheeks get licked.

Since there's no running water at Yentna Station, mushers shovel snow into dog-food cookers to thaw. As the old joke goes, "There is no running water unless you run to get it."

It takes a heap of melted snow to yield enough water to fill the cooker. Several bottles of heating fuel are used to keep the flame high. Dog food thaws quickly after it's dropped into boiling water.

This hearty meal will contain lots of fat and protein: beef, lamb, turkey, chicken, or liver, and sometimes even beaver, moose, caribou, or seal meat. Some mushers

32

Opposite: *A musher's meal is prepared in the dark and cold of an Alaskan night in February.*

Below: *A hearty meal is the perfect reward for the start of a job well done.*

serve dinner on flat cooking pans similar to baking sheets; others use metal bowls.

Not everything is hauled to Yentna by sled. An additional 4 pounds (1.8 kilograms) of dog food per dog is flown to the layover before the race, packed in heavy bags, and tied with rope. The large amount of food is a safeguard in case bad weather keeps dropped dogs from being flown out for a few days.

Mushers munch on trail mix, salmon jerky, or other snacks while waiting for their own dinners to cook: sealed plastic bags of chili, stew, or pasta. Dropped in boiling water, the bags also double as bowls. A whole pizza can thaw over the high blue flame.

Equipment damage is repaired and chewed harnesses are mended—all under the light of the mushers' headlamps. When the mushers finish with their

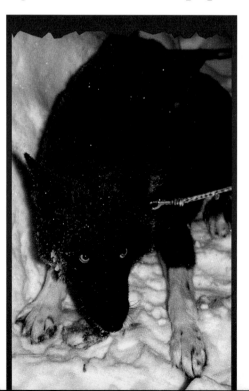

Opposite: *Sleep is essential, but sometimes hard to come by. Even though they have trained well for the race, the young mushers find it a tough, but exciting, challenge.*

Below: *Before a musher can rest, equipment must be checked and, if necessary, repaired.*

chores, they gather around the bonfire built earlier by the owners of Yentna Station. Munching homemade cookies, the mushers share hair-raising stories of gale-force blasts, runaway teams, tangled lines, wrong turns, narrow ice bridges, and ice holes with sucking overflow water.

Even though bleary-eyed from cold and exhaustion, few mushers get more than a couple of hours of sleep. Some empty their sled bag, then push their sleeping bag inside. Others throw their

sleeping bag on the straw next to their team. Dogs radiate warmth, as they sleep curled in a ball with their tails laid across their faces.

For the mushers, sweet dreams are lost to a rehashing of the day's mistakes and visions of the return 75-mile (120-kilometer) trip to Wasilla. The hardest part is knowing that plans will probably have to be scrapped because of poor trail conditions, unpredictable weather, equipment breakdowns, and maybe even dog problems.

All too soon an alarm buzzes the first wake-up. The first team to go is fed and watered, its necklines and tuglines checked, and sled bag repacked. Finally, the racing bib is slipped over the musher's parka. Race officials set their own alarms and gather in a 4 A.M. snowfall, ready to send the first musher back down the trail to Wasilla and the finish line.

Every musher who completes the Jr. Iditarod is honored with a special finisher's patch and trophy at the awards ceremony. Special awards are also given for Sportsmanship, Rookie of the Year, the best lead dog (the Blue Harness award) and the best-cared-for team (the Humanitarian award, which is given by the head veterinarian). According

38

Below: It takes daring and hard work to compete in the Jr. Iditarod, and as the smile on this musher's face shows, participating is something to be proud of.

to tradition, the Red Lantern goes to the last musher to cross the finish line. Meant to light the way home, the lantern has become a symbol of "stick-to-itiveness."

The first to cross the finish line, the winner receives a round-trip airplane ticket to Nome for presentation of the first-place trophy at the Musher's Banquet following the end of the famed Iditarod Trail Sled Dog Race.

No matter where the mushers finish in the Jr. Iditarod, each young competitor has achieved a notable feat that few dare to undertake. All of them have gone the distance and established themselves and their teams in the annals of Iditarod lore.

Like the finisher's patch sewn on the parkas, memories of the adventure and feelings of accomplishment will be stitched forever in their minds.

40

Idita-Talk

Basket sled — a sled with its basket raised off the snow on short, upright posts.

Booties — socks that protect a dog's feet from the snow and ice. Different types of materials are used to make them: polar fleece, trigger cloth, denim, and nylon.

Checker — a race official who checks each team in and out of designated checkpoints. Mandatory gear is also checked.

Checkpoint — a specific spot along the race trail where a musher must sign in and out. Mandatory gear is checked by a race official.

Dog box — a camperlike shell with individual cubbyholes that fits on the back of a pickup truck and is used to carry dogs.

Double lead — two dogs in front of the team who lead side by side.

Drag brake — a flat metal device attached to the back of the sled with claws on the bottom side. The musher steps on the brake to slow the team.

Dropped dog — a dog that is tired or injured and "dropped" from the race. A veterinarian cares for dropped dogs at the checkpoint. After the race these dogs are flown back to Wasilla in a bush plane.

Front-runner — the leader in a race or other competition.

Gangline — the main line that runs through the center of the team and attaches to the sled. Each dog is joined to the gangline by the tugline (snapped to the back of the harness) and neckline (snapped to the collar).

"Gee!" — the command to turn right.

Handler — a person who helps a musher with the daily care and training of sled dogs.

Harness — a device that fits over the dog's shoulders and along its back, putting the pulling power in the lines. Race rules require that the neck and breast panel of all harnesses be padded. Six inches (15 centimeters) of reflector tape must be visible on each harness.

"Haw!" — the command to turn left.

Husky — the general term for any northern-type dog.

Lead dog — a dog that runs in the front position. It must be both smart and fast.

"Let's go!", "Hike!", "All right!", "Mush!" — commands for the team to start moving. "Mush" is thought to come from the French word *marchon*, a command used by early French dog drivers that means "to walk."

"Line out!" — the command to the lead dog to pull the team straight out from the sled. It's used when a musher is hooking or unhooking the team.

Mandatory gear — according to race rules, mushers must carry in the sled certain items to ensure quality care and safety for themselves and their dogs.

Mandatory layover — a required rest period taken at a certain checkpoint.

Musher — a person who drives a team of dogs.

Neckline — a short line that connects the dog's collar to the gangline.

Pedaling — a one-foot push that mushers use to help move the sled forward.

Rookie — a musher participating in the Jr. Iditarod for the first time.

Runners — two long bottom pieces of the sled that come in contact with the snow. Mushers stand on the part of the runners that extends behind the basket.

Sled bag — a cloth sack that fits into the sled basket and holds the load.

Snow hook — a heavy piece of metal with two U-shaped prongs attached to the snub line. Hooked around a tree or stuck in ice, it's used to anchor the team for a short time.

Snub line — a rope attached to the sled. It's used to secure the sled to a stationary object such as a tree.

44

Swing dogs — two dogs hooked up behind the lead dogs. They help "swing" the team around curves.

Tail-ender — the team in the last position of the race.

Team dogs — dogs in the main body of the team; other than the lead, swing, or wheel dogs.

"Trail!" — a call by a musher asking for the right-of-way to overtake another team.

Trailbreakers — volunteers who travel by snow machine to clear and mark a trail for the race.

Tugline — a line that joins the back part of the dog's harness to the gangline; also called the "backline."

Wheel dogs — the two dogs directly in front of the sled. These dogs are trained to pull the sled around corners and trees.

"Whoa!" — a call for the team to stop. It's often used with pressure on the drag brake.

Index

Alaskan husky, 8
Alaska Railroad Hospital, Anchorage, 5
"All right!" command, 11
Anchorage, Alaska, 5, 6
Awards and trophies, 38, 40

Basket sleds, 16
Blizzards, 14
Blue Harness award, 38
Booties, 23, 25
Boots, 18

Cassette players, 21, 26
Checkpoints, 23, 28

Dog box, 11
Dog food, 12, 21-24, 26, 32
Dog sled transportation, 5-6
Drag brake, 23
Dropped dogs, 21, 28, 31, 34

Equipment repair, 34

Flat Horn Lake, 20, 23
Front-runners, 28

Ganglines, 12
Gear list, 21
"Gee" command, 20
Gloves, 18
Gold rush, 6

Harnesses, 11, 12
"Haw" command, 20
Headlamps, 28, 34
Health certificates, 14
Heat packs, 18
"Hike!" command, 11, 20
Honeyballs, 24
Humanitarian award, 38
Hydration, 24

Iditarod National Historic Trail, 20
Iditarod Trail Sled Dog Race, 6, 40
Immunization records, 14
Lake Lucille, 16
Lead dogs, 20, 38

Mandatory gear, 21, 23
Marchon, 20
Medical treatment, 31
Moose, 16-18
"Mush!" command, 20
Musher's Banquet, 40

Neck gaiters, 18
Necklines, 12, 38
Nenana, Alaska, 5
Nome, Alaska, 5, 6

Pass-through checkpoint, 23

Race marshal, 28
Racing bibs, 6, 12
Red Lantern award, 40
Rookie of the Year award, 38
Rookies, 8, 14
Runners, 18, 26

Serum run (1925), 5-6
Sled bags, 11, 28, 36, 38
Sleep, 36
Snow hook, 18
Snub lines, 31
Sportsmanship award, 38
Susitna River, 26

Tail-enders, 28
Temperatures, 14, 24, 25
Trailbreakers, 14
Trail conditions, 16, 36
Trail markers, 14, 23
Tuglines, 12, 38

Verbal commands, 20, 23
Veterans, 8, 14
Veterinarians, 11, 31, 38

Wasilla, Alaska, 12
Weather conditions, 14, 36
"Whoa!" command, 23
Winds, 14

Yentna River, 26
Yentna Station Roadhouse, 16, 26, 28, 29, 31-32, 36

About the Author

As part of her research for this book, author and photographer Sherry Shahan rode in a dogsled for the first part of the Iditarod Trail Sled Dog Race in Alaska. Other assignments have taken her on horseback into Africa's Maasailand and hiking in a leech-infested rain forest in Australia. And those are just the A's.

Her travel articles and photographs have appeared in scores of international, national, and regional publications. She is also the author and photo-illustrator of several books for young readers, including *Barnacles Eat With Their Feet: Delicious Facts About the Tide Pool Food Chain*, for The Millbrook Press.

When not on an exciting assignment, she shoots wildlife photographs near her home on California's central coast.